W9-BXY-865

Queen Elizabeth II
The World's Longest-Reigning Monarch

by Grace Hansen

Abdo
HISTORY MAKER
BIOGRAPHIES
Kids

abdopublishing.com

Published by Abdo Kids, a division of ABDO, P.O. Box 398166, Minneapolis, Minnesota 55439.
Copyright © 2018 by Abdo Consulting Group, Inc. International copyrights reserved in all countries.
No part of this book may be reproduced in any form without written permission from the publisher.
Abdo Kids Jumbo™ is a trademark and logo of Abdo Kids.

Printed in the United States of America, North Mankato, Minnesota.

102017

012018

3 1907 00395 4137

THIS BOOK CONTAINS
RECYCLED MATERIALS

Photo Credits: Alamy, AP Images, Getty Images, iStock, Shutterstock

Production Contributors: Teddy Borth, Jennie Forsberg, Grace Hansen

Design Contributors: Dorothy Toth, Laura Mitchell

Publisher's Cataloging in Publication Data

Names: Hansen, Grace, author.

Title: Queen Elizabeth II: the world's longest-reigning monarch / by Grace Hansen.

Other titles: The world's longest-reigning monarch

Description: Minneapolis, Minnesota : Abdo Kids, 2018. | Series: History maker biographies |
    Includes glossary, index and online resource (page 24).

Identifiers: LCCN 2017943162 | ISBN 9781532104299 (lib.bdg.) | ISBN 9781532105418 (ebook) |
    ISBN 9781532105975 (Read-to-me ebook)

Subjects: LCSH: Elizabeth--II,--Queen of Great Britain,--1926- --Juvenile literature. | Great Britain--Kings,
    queens and rulers--Biography--Juvenile literature. | Queens--Great Britain--Biography--Juvenile
    literature.

Classification: DDC 941.085092 [B]--dc23

LC record available at https://lccn.loc.gov/2017943162

Table of Contents

Early Years

Queen Elizabeth was born on April 21, 1926. She was a princess then. Little did her family know that she would one day be Queen of Great Britain.

United Kingdom

Elizabeth's grandfather died in 1936. Her uncle was made king. But King Edward III did not want the crown. Her father became king instead. He took the name King George VI.

Elizabeth took on many **responsibilities**. During World War II, she hosted radio broadcasts. She comforted Britain's children with her words. She was only 14 years old.

In 1947, Elizabeth married Phillip Mountbatten. They would have four children together.

King George VI died in 1952.
This made Elizabeth the ruling
monarch. Her **coronation** was
on June 2, 1953.

13

The Young Queen

Elizabeth had many duties.
One was to meet with Winston
Churchill each week. He was the
Prime Minister. He updated her
on political matters.

Queen Elizabeth also traveled a great deal. She visited Britain's **Commonwealth**.

16

17

Sapphire Jubilee

February 6, 2017, marked 65 years as queen. Elizabeth had a quiet day. She spent it thinking of her late father.

Elizabeth is known for her strength and grace. She is loved by her people and family. She is respected around the world.

Timeline

Elizabeth's father, Albert becomes King George VI.

Elizabeth marries Phillip Mountbatten. They later have four children together.

After her **coronation**, Elizabeth goes on her first **Commonwealth** country tour.

The Queen becomes the longest reigning British **monarch** with 65 years on the throne.

1936

1947

1953

2017

1926

1940

1952

2016

April 21
Princess Elizabeth Alexandra Mary is born in London, England.

Elizabeth gives her first broadcast during the Children's Hour radio program.

King George VI dies, making Elizabeth Queen of the United Kingdom at 25 years old.

October
The king of Thailand dies, making Elizabeth the longest-reigning monarch alive.

Glossary

Commonwealth – a grouping of 52 member states that are mostly former territories of the British Empire and are lead by the English monarch.

coronation – the ceremony at which a king or queen is officially crowned.

monarch – a ruler such as a king, queen, or emperor.

Prime Minister – a chief minister and head of a government with a parliament.

responsibility – a duty or task that you should do because it is right or required.

23

Index

Abdo Kids
ONLINE
FREE! ONLINE MULTIMEDIA RESOURCES

Visit **abdokids.com** and use this code to access crafts, games, videos, and more!

Abdo Kids Code:

HQK4299